A Fool's Journey

*...Spiritual and Lyrical Reflections
of a Man Remade by God*

Jeff Chacon

ILLUMINATION PUBLISHERS

A Fool's Journey—Spiritual and Lyrical Reflections of a Man Remade by God

ISBN: 978-1-958723-41-8. Copyright © 2024 by Jeff Chacon.

Illumination Publishers International titles may be purchased in bulk for classroom instruction, business, fund-raising, or sales promotional use. For information, please e-mail us at info@ipibooks.com. We care deeply about using renewable resources and uses recycled paper whenever possible.

All Scripture quotations, unless otherwise indicated, are from The Holy Bible, New International Version, Copyright © 1973, 1978, 1984, 2011 by Biblica, Inc. Used by permission. All rights reserved worldwide.

Interior layout: Toney Mulhollan. Cover design by Jeff Chacon.

About the author: Jeff Chacon served in the full-time ministry for 36 years before retiring in 2022, and now serves as an elder for the Anchor Point Church in Tampa, Florida. Jeff and his wife, Lisa, are probably  most well known for their marriage and family workshops, as well as Jeff's first book, *Dare to Dream Again*. They have three amazing sons, three wonderful daughters-in-law, and eight adorable grandchildren.

What others are saying about this book…

"Wow! I can hardly find words for this. I was brought to tears many times. Jeff is vulnerable, honest, deep, genuine, transparent, inspirational, and creative. Most of all, he shows us what an authentic relationship/daily walk with God over decades looks like."

—LauriAnne Conkling
Women's Ministry Leader, Anchor Point Church

"I love this book! It will be helpful to all disciples but especially husbands and fathers. Also, ministers will connect with the book as Jeff shares his ups and downs of faith."

—Gregg Marutzky , ICOC Teacher, MDiv, PhD

"I enjoyed very much reading this book. My old friend, Jeff Chacon, has a gift of communicating. He and I share that gift and often express it in similar ways. However, he has a way of communicating that I do not have—through poetry. Poetic expression reaches a part of our soul that nothing else does. Today I read his book of poetry and saw his soul."

—Gordon Ferguson
Author of 19 books on the Christian life and leadership

"This is unlike any memoir you've ever read (and not just because half of it is written in poetry). Read it slowly. Every section is worthy of meditation and prayer. Jeff's vulnerability will draw your own heart out. I'm sure this special book will strengthen your faith, encourage your heart, and bless your soul. That's what it did for me."

—Linda Brumley, author of *My Beggar's Purse, Love, Laughter and Law* and *Called to Be Holy*

"This is a beautiful piece of writing on the journey of life with Jesus. It has blessed me and caused me to value the ups and downs of life with Jesus as my Lord."

—Rob Zabala
Elder, We Are Church, Crazy Love Ministries

"*Jeff Chacon's book,* A Fool's Journey: Spiritual and Lyrical Reflections of a Man Remade by God, *is a surprising work that moved me on an emotional level. And based on who I know Jeff to be, this makes perfect sense. What I appreciate about him is that he is laser-focused on the care of our hearts before God. This makes him a true shepherd.*

In a world that asks, "what do I need to learn to change this problem as soon as possible?" Jeff Chacon's book serves as a philosophical affront to our insatiable propensity to fix, influence, and even cajole ourselves into acceptability before God. Instead, he uses poetry to interface directly with our hearts.

Jeff's book is a gift of vulnerability and faith that always points toward our loving Father. I can't recommend it highly enough!"

—Dr. Sean St. Jean
Author of "*Spiritual Trauma: A Guide For Healing Your Heart From Church Hurts*"

Contents

Contents

Contents

Dedication

To my friend, John Godwin,
who led me to Christ,
taught me how to pray,
and taught me how to
lay down my life
for others.

I'm eternally indebted to you, John.

Foreword

Welcome, dear reader, to a journey unlike any other. Within these pages, you will encounter the soul-stirring poetry and profound reflections of a man who has devoted his life to seeking God. His words are not merely ink on paper but echoes of a heart ablaze with love for the divine.

In a world where the noise of everyday life often drowns out the whisper of the spirit, his poetry serves as a beacon of light, guiding us back to the source of all existence. With each verse, he invites us to pause, reflect, and reconnect with that source.

But this book is more than just a collection of poems; it chronicles a spiritual journey marked by moments of doubt, revelation, darkness, and light.

In the following pages, you will embark on a profound journey into the depths of one man's soul. Through the lens of poetry, he has captured the essence of his spiritual quest, weaving together words that resonate with the very heartbeat of the universe. Each verse reflects his innermost thoughts, a glimpse into the mysteries of the soul, and an invitation to explore the infinite depths of spirituality. He is, for us, a pioneer, a guide, mapping out the journey ahead.

Jeff Chacon and I have been best friends since our days in college together, when he led me to Christ in 1983. I love and respect him so much. He is a man, a brother, a husband, a father, an evangelist, and an elder in God's kingdom. He is one man, and he is every man. He is me, and he is you.

As you turn the pages of this book, may you be uplifted by the beauty of his prose, enlightened by the wisdom of his insights, and inspired to traverse your own journey of self-discovery and spiritual growth.

—Robert Carrillo MDiv.
Teacher, Evangelist, Instructor Rocky Mountain School of Ministry and Theology
Founder of The Way Ministry

As a person who has spent most of my life preaching the Gospel of Jesus from the pulpit, this book represents a much-needed articulation of the greatest story ever told, from the heart. In a religious world where the Gospel is explained with lofty theological concepts or multiple and varied theories of atonement, Jeff illustrates it in the same simple but profound way those around Jesus did—with a transformed life, from the inside out.

This story of a changed life is not just Jeff's, it ours, too.

A Fool's Journey reminds me of the classic I read as a young man, *The Pilgrim's Progress.* In it, John Bunyan illustrated the reality of the Christian walk, through allegory, by detailing all the tendencies of the human heart—pleasure, legalism, duty, seeking worldly wisdom, even getting stuck in periods of doubt and spiritual loneliness.

However, Jeff's work here is not allegory, it is real life. All of life–ups, downs, sin, joy, despondency, doubt, bondage, freedom, and so much more. This collection of poetry and life experience has helped me understand all phases of the Christian life. I believe it can fill you with inspiration as a young and fresh seeker, but also fill you with hope as an older and seasoned Christian.

I am positive you will be blessed by reading this book. I count myself blessed for knowing the man behind this book. Jeff Chacon is an authentic Christian who has been through everything! Through all of his experiences, he has emerged a joyful and grace-filled Christian. He is a true friend, a patient mentor, a deep theological thinker, a person who exemplifies Jesus to those he interacts with.

In our short time here on earth, it is our calling as Christians to use everything we have to point people to the transformative power of the Gospel. I am grateful Jeff has shared, in this powerful and vulnerable work, the way to true spiritual meaning in a fallen and confused world: let Jesus change you, wherever you are and whatever you are going through.

I pray this book blesses you, helps you grow, and opens your heart to deeper realizations and discoveries than can ever be explained from the pulpit.

—Daren Overstreet
Senior Minister, Anchor Point Church in Tampa FL
Masters in Missional Leadership
Founder and Director of Biblicallyresilient.com

Opening

"Brothers and sisters, think of what you were when you were called. Not many of you were wise by human standards; not many were influential; not many were of noble birth. [27]But God chose the foolish things of the world to shame the wise; God chose the weak things of the world to shame the strong. [28]God chose the lowly things of this world and the despised things—and the things that are not—to nullify the things that are, [29]so that no one may boast before him. [30]It is because of him that you are in Christ Jesus, who has become for us wisdom from God—that is, our righteousness, holiness, and redemption. [31]Therefore, as it is written:

"Let the one who boasts boast in the Lord."
(1 Corinthians 1:26-31)

Remade by God

Jeff Chacon

(2022)

The fool has been given wisdom from above.
The selfish man has been transformed by the power of love.
And the fearful man has been given the courage of
the lion of Judah.

And in his temple, all cry,
"Glory to God!"

"Therefore, as it is written:
"Let the one who boasts boast in the Lord."

Preface

That opening scripture describes my life. I am a fool and I am weak. I don't say that to sound falsely humble. I say that because it's true. And the poetry in this book will make that abundantly clear.

God took one of the least likely people imaginable—a partying, shallow, pleasure-seeker—and not only saved me, but healed me, and radically transformed me from the inside out. And like the Apostle Paul said, if God can do that with someone like me, then he can surely do it for you too. (1 Timothy 1:15-17, paraphrased).

I'm 64 years old and retired as I write this, which gives me the time and inclination to reflect a bit over the years. And as I look back on my life, I see God's shaping hands all over it—even when I was furthest from him—which totally astonishes, humbles, and amazes me.

And few things show God's hand more in my life than the poems I frequently wrote out of my anguish, confusion, or joy. I don't know why, but for some reason I wrote and kept these poems from the time I was a worldly teenager to the present day, producing a kind of lyrical record of my spiritual life.

Some of these poems are pretty raw; others are intimate and vulnerable. Believe me, I never intended to publish most of them. But they're real and authentic, and I think you'll be able to relate to most of them. I put the best ones in chronological order, organized them by theme, and decided now was the time to glorify God by showing what he could do in the life of a fool like me.

I hope my honest reflections throughout this book, and the heartfelt poetry that has punctuated my life, will be an enjoyable source of encouragement and inspiration for you.

And may God be glorified by the book he has written with my life.

—Jeff Chacon

Introduction

The poems in this book will help you see how I got here, but let's start with this one, written fairly recently. It's one of my favorites because it describes the person I desperately want to be each day. I wrote this heartfelt manifesto six years ago, and I often read it to start my times with the Lord in the morning. I hope it expresses your own aspirations as well, and helps you to not only believe in God, but to truly be in love with him.

> *"One thing I ask from the Lord,*
> *this only do I seek:*
> *that I may dwell in the house of the Lord*
> *all the days of my life,*
> *to gaze on the beauty of the Lord*
> *and to seek him in his temple."*
> (Psalm 27:4)

I want to be in love with God
(2018)

I don't want religion—I want relationship.
I don't want rules—I want romance.
I don't want to just believe in God—I want to be in love with God.

I want to wake up each morning and be delighted with the thought of God.
I want to quickly get to my favorite prayer spot, anticipating something special and new each morning.

I want to dig into my Bible like a treasure hunter looking for gold.
I want to pray like David—passionate about everything, wrestling with my heart, and constantly trying to claw my way into the next dimension.

I don't want to go through life alone.
I want to go through life with Him.

I don't want to waste my time on earth.
I want to make every moment count.

I don't want to be drawn to the pleasures of this world.
I want to be allured by the lover of my soul.

I don't want to worry—I want to pray.
I don't want to fear—I want to trust.
I don't want to hope—I want to know.

I don't want to live for myself—I want to live for others.
I don't want to seek diversion—I want to seek conversions.
I don't want to be temporarily wealthy—I want to be eternally rich.

I don't want to be like the world—I want to be like my Lord.
I don't want to fit in—I want to stand out.
I don't want to make myself comfortable—I want to make myself useful.

I don't want religion… I want relationship.
I don't want rules… I want romance.
I don't want to just believe in God… I want to be in love with God.

Chapter One:

Ignorant Bliss

Pre-Christian Days
High School, 1976 – 1978

Rewind to my life before I was a Christian who loves God. At sixteen years old, I was a classic fool: walking in the wrong direction, oblivious to danger, and mistakenly thinking I had it all figured out. I epitomized the description of a fool in the book of Proverbs...

"Do you see a person wise in their own eyes?
There is more hope for a fool than for them."
(Proverbs 26:12)

"Wine is a mocker and beer a brawler;
whoever is led astray by them is not wise."
(Proverbs 20:1)

Here's what I wrote when I was 16 years old. Behold, the fool…

Marco, Mires and Chico
(1976, 16 years old)

Ho! Ho! Ho! to the bottle I go
to heal my heart and drown my woe.
Rain may fall and wind may blow
and many miles be still to go,
but under a tall tree I will lie
and let the clouds go sailing by.

Ho! Ho! Ho! to the bottle I go
to heal my heart and drown my woe.
Lost my job, my car's in tow,
got a girlfriend that won't let go,
but upon this sidewalk I will lie
and watch the cars go driving by.

Ho! Ho! Ho! to the bottle I go
to heal my heart and drown my woe.
Michelob's the beer we drink,
it helps our minds go on the blink,
so without worry we three can cruise
while all you fools are singing the blues.

Some people hated high school; I loved it. My friends and I were kings of our small-town high school—at least in our own minds. But when we graduated, we became yesterday's news. This piece was written just months after I graduated from high school and wrestles with that feeling of no longer mattering, and wishing we were somebody again. The next chapter of poems will painfully illustrate my growing emptiness inside, but I think it all started here, because at some point, the party has to end—and then what are you left with?

"I said to myself,
'Come now, I will test you with pleasure
to find out what is good.'
But that also proved to be meaningless."
(Ecclesiastes 2:1)

The Days of Love and Football
(1978, 18 years old)

Round up the boys!
Get at least three or four!
We'll have a few beers,
then drink a few more.

It was Thanksgiving weekend
and the boys were in town.
We'd cruise on up Orange
and have a look around.

Well, the party's raged
and the dance was jumpin'.
It was Ladies night
and every girl's heart was thumpin'.

But this year was strange,
it was different and new.
The dance was the same,
but not the crew.

It was their turn now
(the class of '79 and '80)
to impress their dates
with dinner at Mulvaney's.

And the two on the floor
with the classic style
were neither Mark and Jeff
nor John and Kyle.

They were this year's seniors
named Kelly and Joe;
it was their turn now
to put on the show.

So, we cruised around town
looking for something radical and cool
and we ended up skinny-dipping
in the Muni pool.

Well, it's fun getting chased
by the police of Coronado.
They chase us on foot
and they chase us in autos.

But it's just not the same
as a high school dance.
I miss the good vibes
and all the romance.

We've strut with pride
over the familiar campus turf,
and played the games of love and football
in the city by the surf.

We've had our rad nights
and our days in the sun,
and it hurts now to watch
as the others have fun.

Our sun has set;
into the night we have been swept.
And our new sun will not shine
until we have slept.

But time is like sand;
it slips through our fingers.
And though life goes on,
one thought yet lingers:

that tomorrow's sun
will not be like today's;
nor will there ever be a light so bright
as the sweet memory of yesterday's.

Chapter Two:

Feeling Lost

Pre-Christian Days
College, 1979 – 1980

*L*ife seemed easy for me as a teenager with not much parental supervision. Problems? Drink them away. But after high school the realities of life were catching up with me. Life was getting harder, and the drinking, drugs, and partying could no longer dull me enough to make my problems go away. I had to deal with reality—and I had no idea where to start.

This poem was written after I got the news that my older brother Paul's marriage of six months had just ended with her walking out on him. It shook me because we were "a good family" in our minds, and I never imagined the house of cards could come crashing down so quickly. But at 19 years old, my world was falling apart…and this was just the beginning.

*"But the way of the wicked is like deep darkness;
they do not know what makes them stumble."*
(Proverbs 4:19)

Confusion

(1979, 19 years old)

Bewilderment.
I'm shaken.
My world is shaken.

Suddenly my head's not all there.
It was—before tonight.
Now, I'm not sure anymore.

Childhood, life, marriage, life, retirement, life, death.
But have we lived?
Or is this an illusion?

Death will tell us…
Or will he?

Sickness-health, love-hate, war-peace, boy-girl!
Compliments? Contradictions?! Lies?!

Confusion.

Life.

After high school, I took a gap-year job as a desk clerk at the iconic Hotel Del Coronado. It was a beach resort hotel that fit my escapist mentality. But one day a man unexpectedly died right there in the lobby where I worked. I didn't know him, but the shock of a life ending so abruptly in front of me made me think about my pleasure-seeking lifestyle and where it was all heading. It was a wakeup call that I desperately needed.

"While people are saying, 'Peace and safety,'
destruction will come on them suddenly,
as labor pains on a pregnant woman,
and they will not escape."
(1 Thessalonians 5:3)

A Man Died Today at the Del
(1979, 19 years old)

A man died today at the Del.

I had a champagne brunch
in La Jolla this morning
and got drunk.

I spent last night drinking beer
and fooling around
with another hotel guest
till five in the morning.

I didn't even know her name.

A man died today at the Del.

*B*y the time I went to college and continued my partying ways I was growing increasingly desperate inside. The emptiness of my life was overtaking me like the stifling heat of an endless desert with no water in sight. Years later, I would resonate with the profound reflection of Henry David Thoreau when he observed, *"The mass of men lead lives of quiet desperation. What is called resignation is confirmed desperation."* My life was built on sand, and when the inevitable storms of life came, it fell with a great crash. My baseless optimism had finally given way to the cynical reality of a life without God. I finally hit bottom, and the pain was excruciating.

> *"But everyone who hears these words of mine*
> *and does not put them into practice*
> *is like a foolish man who built his house on sand.*
> *[27]The rain came down, the streams rose,*
> *and the winds blew and beat against that house,*
> *and it fell with a great crash."*
> (Matthew 7:26-27)

Despair
(1980, 20 years old)

It's a game,
it's the same
as a rat lookin' for cheese.

Push a button,
pop a pill,
and do whatever you please.

Cuz you're as common as disease
and as welcome as a sneeze.

Don't you know that you are no one
and that no one really cares?!

You were born into desire
and will die out of despair.

HEY LISTEN!

No one gives you nothin'
and no one really cares.

Chapter Three:

New Life

Early Christian Days
College, 1981 – 1983

For nine months I had recurring night-mares of completely losing control, and would fall to my knees every night before going to bed in my dorm room with one desperate cry: "God, I don't know you, but please, help!" God heard me the first time, but he was waiting for the natural results of my sin to crush the pride out of me first. When the time was right, he sent a faithful servant of his, named John Godwin, to invite me to his small group Bible study, and after three months I repented of my sins and made a lifelong commitment to follow Jesus. The recurring nightmares stopped and were replaced with a deep peace. I've always thought this Psalm summarized my conversion best:

*"Some became fools
through their rebellious ways
and suffered affliction
because of their iniquities.*

¹⁸They loathed all food
and drew near the gates of death.
¹⁹Then they cried to the Lord in their trouble,
and he saved them from their distress.
²⁰He sent out his word and healed them;
he rescued them from the grave.
²¹Let them give thanks to the Lord
for his unfailing love
and his wonderful deeds for mankind.
²²Let them sacrifice thank offerings
and tell of his works with songs of joy."
(Psalm 107:17-22)

God saved a fool like me, and I'll spend the rest of my life thanking him for it. This poem on the following page reflects the biblical wisdom he began to pour into me, as my eyes would slowly open to the truths of life he would reveal over the next several years...

The Paradox of Life
(1981, 21 years old, one month after my
baptism into Christ)

If you want love,
give it away,
and you will receive it
in abundance.

If you want faith,
act on what little you have,
and it will grow
to be strong.

If you seek truth,
be truthful with yourself,
and God will answer
your prayer.

Be wise my friend,
and always remember
that the paradox of life is:
in dying we live.

*A*fter finding my first love in God, he graciously blessed me with my second love: Lisa Ann Cornelius, the beautiful, pure-hearted, antithesis of me—and the girl I would marry after we graduated college. She brought out the best in me—and still does. Thirty-eight years later, we're more in love than ever. But it all started here, as two young Christians shedding the false selves of our past and finding the child inside of us that God created us to be.

"But Jesus called the children to him and said,
'Let the little children come to me, and do not hinder them,
for the kingdom of God belongs to such as these.'"
(Luke 18:16)

I'm Finding the Child

(1983, 23 years old, written for Lisa while dating)

You're causing my heart
to learn to let go.
And I'm finding the child
that I lost long ago.

I'm finding the child
that's deep inside me.
I'm finding the child
God wants me to be.

When I'm with you I laugh;
When I'm with you I sing.
Your love makes me feel
like I can do anything!

I can run, I can jump,
I can walk on a wall!
I can sing in your ear,
or say nothing at all.

I'm finding the child
I want so badly to be.
I'm finding the child
God loves me to be.

Thank you, Lisa,
for setting me free.
I'm finding the child—
and the child is me.

Chapter Four:

Growing in my Understanding

My 20s and 30s
1984 – 1998

*a*ll growing Christians are inevitably faced with the same false religion that Jesus adamantly opposed in the Pharisees and Teachers of the Law of his day. Man's rules and regulations are inexplicably appealing to our sinful nature. I guess we inherently want to disengage our hearts and put our Christianity on cruise control instead of having to wrestle with our hearts and deal with all of their conflicting passions. But deadening our hearts with legalism is spiritual suicide to God. He desperately desires our genuine affection, and will fight for our love as long as we have breath. This is one of my favorite poems. Soak it up, and let your heart soar with him.

> *"Therefore I am now going to allure her;*
> *I will lead her into the wilderness*
> *and speak tenderly to her.*

…¹⁶"In that day," declares the Lord,
"you will call me 'my husband';
you will no longer call me 'my master.'"
(Hosea 2:14,16)

It's All About Love
(1992, 32 years old)

They run after pleasure
and we call it sin.
We run after favor
and never get in.

And the prophets howl,
while the wise man cries:
"It's all about love,
and the rest is all lies."

"Stop trusting in your good,"
God says to us all.
"The best of them tried,
and hit the same wall.

Give me your hand.
Then give me your heart.
We'll head for the sky,
and that's just the start!

Shut your eyes tight—
don't look (if you dare)—
Then jump in my arms
and swim in my care.

What do I want?
Do you really have to ask?
What can man do?
What performance, what task?

I want what's of value
but just can't be bought.
I want the one thing
even God's not got.

I want you to want me
more than life itself;
more than food or pleasure
or even your health.

I want you to think of me
morning, noon and night.
And I want you to call
and I want you to write.

I've always wanted you!
Oh, why can't you see?
And now I want you
to always want me."

And the prophets howl,
while the wise man cries:
"It's all about love,
and the rest is all lies."

*a*s I grew closer to God, I got more in touch with my upbringing and the things that I missed growing up. I love my father and admire him greatly for his service to the community, but his job took him away from the family for long periods of time, which left a hole in my heart. With the help of a trained counselor, I processed that hurt in my early 30s and wrote this healing poem. I offer it here for all who had a distant, difficult, or non-existent relationship with their fathers. Feel the hope our truest father gives us.

> *"I will be a Father to you,*
> *and you will be my sons and daughters,*
> *says the Lord Almighty."*
> (2 Corinthians 6:18)

"We Never Played Catch"
(1992, 32 years old)

We never played catch
or tried to walk on a wall.
He didn't come to my games
when I used to play football.

All I wish was I knew him,
and that he knew me.
But now it's too late –
I'm almost 33.

No, not too late,
because there really are three.
There's three dads now:
My dad, my God, and me!

To my three children
I'm the one they see.
So, the past is now the present;
and the future's up to me!

Cool! We'll play catch, we'll have fun,
And we'll talk all the time!
Yeah, most of all…
we'll spend a lot of time.
And we all have God.

So, there is justice you see,
because everyone can have
the perfect Daddy.

He's loving and loyal,
and where He really shines,
is He's really good
at just "spending time."

I forgive you Dad;
as I hope my kids forgive me.
And I thank you, Father,
for giving me three.

---

a friend of mine in ministry was regularly getting passed over for ministry roles and came to me with his heartache. It's not that he wanted a position or title; it's just that he wanted to find his place in the church. "What's my role in this whole cosmic drama God is orchestrating from above? Where do I fit in?" Maybe you've asked those same questions. Here's the poem I wrote for him. I hope it ministers to your heart as well.

"What, after all, is Apollos? And what is Paul?
Only servants, through whom you came to believe—
as the Lord has assigned to each his task."
(1 Corinthians 3:5)

The Question
(1998, 38 years old)

Who knows, who cares, who wonders who they'll be
when life is a lark and all is carefree?

But something changes deep inside
when the Great One calls and there's nowhere to hide.

First fear, then resistance, then soon we give in.
And the question is born: "Where do I fit in?"

I asked for a sword, and was given a towel.
I asked to lead and was told to follow.

So, I followed closely and gave my heart.
I washed feet that were dirty and did my part.

And there were times of blessing that could not be denied,
and times of testing when I cried and cried.

Then one day it was over in the twinkling of an eye,
and all that were dead were again alive.

And the Great One came to the back of the line
and said, "You come first. You there, you're mine."

Then the towel in my hand became a great sword
with the words in blood: "Jesus is Lord!"

And the question was answered: "Where do I fit in?"
I'm a humble servant, a servant of him.

Chapter Five:

Processing Hurt by Other Christians

My late 30s and beyond
1999 – Present

I will bet some of you turned to this chapter as soon as you saw it on the Content page. I get it. I probably would have to. It's so important to learn how to process hurt caused by others in the church. I've come to believe that unjust suffering is not only common, but an indispensable class in God's school of transformation. There are deep levels of spirituality and fellowship with our Lord that can only be accessed through unjust suffering. Here is the main scripture that helps me process my hurt with God, followed by a poem that illustrates my struggle.

*"To this you were called, because Christ suffered for you,
leaving you an example, that you should follow in his steps.*
²²'He committed no sin, and no deceit was found in his mouth.'
*²³When they hurled their insults at him, he did not retaliate;
when he suffered, he made no threats.*
Instead, he entrusted himself to him who judges justly."
(1 Peter 2:21-23)

He Knows
(1999, 39 years old)

Me: Did you see that hurtful thing he just did to me?
My conscience: I saw it—and so did God, who feels with you.
But you've got to focus on your response.

Yeah, but he hurt me without cause! That's so unfair!
Yes, but while you're focused on him, God is focused on your
response to him.

Yeah, but what he did was so wrong!
Yes, but how you handle it is what's important now.

Yeah, but he really hurt me!
You're still focused on the wrong person.

Okay… you're right.
I won't retaliate, hate, or hold a grudge.
But does anyone know what I'm going through?
I feel so alone in my suffering.
Jesus knows and understands.
He endured much, much worse.
Remember the cross?

Yes, I remember now.
That helps.
He must know what I'm going through.

Jesus: Yes, I know.

Wow… he really does know.

I do not want to be too specific with names, dates, and places on this one, so I'll simply tell you that the occasion of this poem was the darkest valley I've ever walked through in my life. I was framed and blamed for something I didn't do by someone I trusted. And even worse than being stabbed in the back was the way this individual turned all my closest friends against me. It was shocking, horrifying and devastating. Worst of all, I felt utterly and completely alone.

But we're never alone when we walk with God. I poured my heart out to God and prayed along with the Psalmists for many days. And then, one day, on one of those prayer walks, I literally heard this song in my head. It was the Lord singing to me. I know that sounds weird, but I can't deny what happened. I rushed home and wrote down the words to the song he sang to me. And now I pass the song along to you as healing balm for your soul. May it encourage you as much as it encouraged me.

> *"The Lord is close to the brokenhearted*
> *and saves those who are crushed in spirit."*
> (Psalm 34:18)

What If I Were to Tell You

What if I were to tell you
that I love you more than ever?
What if I were to tell you
that you mean that much to me?

What if I were to tell you
that I'm proud of all you've done?
What if I were to tell you
that I'm proud of who you've become?

What if I were to tell you
that the trials are not a mistake?
What if I were to tell you
that I wish I could take your place?

What if I were to tell you
that I know what you're going through?
What if I were to tell you
that I long to show myself to you?

I love you, my darling,
more than you'll ever realize.
I love you, my sweetheart,
as my eyes begin to cry.

One day I'll show you
things you're not permitted to see.

One day you'll see me,
and the truth will set you free!

What if I were to tell you
that I know what you're going through?
What if I were to tell you
that I long to show myself to you?

Sometimes the loneliness of following our Lord and taking unpopular stands can really ache. We all naturally want to fit in and be accepted by others. But Jesus stood out and was not accepted by most, and that's who we're following.

Not being accepted is something we expect from people outside of the church, but experiencing that rejection from our fellow brothers and sisters in the church can be devastating. We shouldn't be surprised, though. Remember the prophets in the Old Testament? It was their fellow countrymen who opposed them the most. Think of the gospels: it was God's people who persecuted Jesus the most. Think of the Apostle Paul: it was the ridicule and rejection of the Corinthian brothers and sisters that caused him so much pain and heartache.

Whether it's the pain of not fitting in with the world, or not fitting in with some in the church—not fitting in is our destiny. And it stinks. But the passage below and the following poem can help you keep going. Read on, and be encouraged…

"All these people were still living by faith when they died. They did not receive the things promised; they only saw them and welcomed them from a distance, admitting that they were foreigners and strangers on earth. [14]People who say such things show that they are looking for a country of their own. [15]If they had been thinking of the country they had left, they would have had opportunity to return. [16]Instead, they were longing for a better country—a heavenly one. Therefore God is not ashamed to be called their God, for he has prepared a city for them."

(Hebrews 11:13-16)

God, Why?
(2022, 62 years old)

God, why am I a man without a country?
You're not. You're part of the heavenly country.

God, why am I a man without a tribe?
You're not. Your tribe is the people of God through the ages.

**God, why am I regularly taking positions
that are controversial and unpopular?**
Because Jesus' positions are often controversial and unpopular.

God, why am I so misunderstood and mischaracterized at times?
Because that's how they treated the prophets before you.

God, why do I doubt myself so often?
All my servants do.

God, why am I so reluctant to lead?
All true leaders are.

God, why can't this be easier?
Because it's not supposed to be.

God, why can't I just be a nice guy that gets along with everyone?
Because Jesus is not a nice guy that gets along with everyone.

Okay, I see your point… But I still don't like it.
You don't have to like it. None of them did.

I feel better that I'm not alone in this.
You're not alone. I am with you.

Thank you.
You're welcome, my son.

Chapter Six:

Writing *Dare to Dream Again*

My early 40s
2001 – 2002

I wrote my first book, *Dare to Dream Again*, in 2002, at the age of 42. I wanted desperately to fight off the complacency that tends to settle like a fog over us at the halfway point in our lives. I felt moved by God to inspire the church to keep fighting, and to get back up every time we fall. Throughout the writing of the book, I was stirred to express myself lyrically, which resulted in several poems. Here are three of them. In this first one, we hear Jesus calling our name when we feel like giving up.

"To the one who is victorious,
I will give some of the hidden manna.
I will also give that person a white stone
with a new name written on it,
known only to the one who receives it."
(Revelation 2:17b)

What Is Your Name?
(from *Dare to Dream Again,* 2002, 42 years old)

We are more than the sum of our failures.
We are more than our latest defeat.
We were crafted for heavenly glory,
where there still is reserved a seat.

Once, all the world was a canvas,
and we held a brush in our hand.
We really believed it was possible:
"Go in and take the land!"

But like our brother, Don Quixote,
the evil one has had his way,
thrusting his sword in our sides,
and then calling it a day!

Can't you hear above the crowd,
the one who still calls your name?
How many defeats doesn't matter—
to him it's all the same.

All that matters
is the quest in your heart.
You've got to finish
what you start!

"Get up, o warrior!"
the angel gallery shouts aloud.
"Take up the sword
and lift your head proud!"

For the fight is not over
until you fail to rise.
Get back up,
and look to the skies!

Your commander still rides,
still faithful and true.
And he's calling your name—
he's calling for you!

I decided early on in my Christian life that if I was going to be a follower of Jesus, I would be the best follower of his that I could possibly be. I would give my all for the one who has given his all for me. In my natural self, I'd much rather go with the flow than stand out from the crowd. But Jesus didn't go with the flow, he cut a path against the crowd, and he's who I'm following, so, that's where I'm going too. But I need inspiration to keep rising to the occasion, and poems like this one rouse me to my feet. If you're like me, this poem will be jet fuel for your soul. Let if fill you up and inspire you to be the greatest warrior for Christ you can possibly be.

"For the eyes of the Lord range throughout the earth
to strengthen those whose hearts
are fully committed to him."
(2 Chronicles 16:9a)

God's Search

(from *Dare to Dream Again*, 2002, 42 years old)

I'm searching for someone
who is willing to believe
that greatness is given
to those who receive.

They must believe once again
that they can run with the horses
and call on God's power
to summon his forces.

I want someone
with a gleam in their eye—
with their feet on the ground
and their head in the sky.

Where is the person
who will forsake all others
for the love of their God
and the sake of their brothers?

Find me the person
who counts everything a loss—
save the message of Jesus
and his death on the cross!

I'm searching for someone
who knows who they are
and will drive out demons
by God's mighty power.

Now I've caught your eye—
are you the one?
Tell me you're willing
to follow my Son.

Are you the person
who is willing to be great—
who will overcome fear
for destiny's sake?

Don't be a victim,
giving Satan the nod.
You're my child—
so be a warrior for God!"

The Christian Life is a love story, set against the backdrop of a great, cosmic battle between good and evil. So many scriptures bear this out—why are we so often oblivious to this epic war we find ourselves in? One reason is surely that our adversary intentionally hides himself and his army of demons from sight so that we underestimate him and fight the wrong battles, with the wrong weapons.

One of the most important battles to fight is the battle to rescue precious souls from captivity. And that requires using the sword of the Spirit and the shield of faith. All conversions to Christ are only by the grace and power of God himself, but he has graciously called us to fight in his service. And when we work together to save one more soul from captivity, it is the sweetest victory of all.

> "...I tell you, there is rejoicing
> in the presence of the angels of God
> over one sinner who repents."
> (Luke 15:10b)

Oh, Victory Sweet!

(from *Dare to Dream Again,* 2002, 42 years old)

A dark night
on canvas, painted bright
with fireworks like
Christmas lights
shooting, streaming
everywhere—
like carousels
at every fair!

At center stands
a Knight of Light
with sword waved high
against the sky
as if to cry:
"Oh, victory sweet!

We vanquished he,
who slain, now lies
beneath my feet!
Prince of Darkness,
strong and sleek—
but tonight, he lies
in crushed defeat!"

"Another day!"
Darkness shouts aloud.
But he can't be heard
above the crowd
of singing saints
encircling he
who, washed, now stands
both clean and free!

And to the chorus
of the crowd
the angels add
their voices loud:
"Another soul is won today!"

While on God's throne,
on the edge of his seat,
God reaches down,
their hands to meet.

And oh the look
in the Master's eyes
when we fight his fight
and the saints baptize!

Chapter Seven:

Marriage and Family

From my mid-20s to my mid-40s
1985 – 2006

I never thought a selfish, pleasure-seeking fool like me could be washed, renewed, and remade into someone so completely different. God didn't just save my soul—he transformed me, gave me a new heart, and filled me with his Spirit. Like Paul told Timothy:

"Here is a trustworthy saying
that deserves full acceptance:
Christ Jesus came into the world to save sinners—
of whom I am the worst.
¹⁶But for that very reason I was shown mercy
so that in me, the worst of sinners,
Christ Jesus might display his immense
patience as an example
for those who would believe in him
and receive eternal life."
(1 Timothy 1:15-16)

*J*f God can do what he's done in my life, he can surely do it in yours as well. So, I offer the following intimate glimpses into my family as evidence of the power and grace of God in the life of a fool like me, so that God may receive the glory he richly deserves.

"For this reason
a man shall leave his father and his mother,
and be joined to his wife;
and they shall become one flesh."
(Genesis 2:24)

One Flesh

(1985, 25 years old, asking Lisa to marry me)

"Alone and okay"
is what I used to say.
"Don't come too near.
What do you mean, fear?"

I'm still afraid—
but there's something else too—
something inside me...
something that's new.

I've been only one—
now I'm one minus you.
And one's not enough—
one longs to be two.

I give you myself,
I give you my life.
Please take me and say...
that you'll be my wife.

these next three poems were written as dedications to each of my three sons and given to them at their baptisms. Lisa and I framed them in shadow boxes and placed an arrow under each of them as a visual reminder of this verse:

"Children are a heritage from the Lord,
offspring a reward from him.
⁴Like arrows in the hands of a warrior
are children born in one's youth."
(Psalm 127:3-4)

Each of my sons is an arrow, fired into the heart of darkness when they joined the spiritual battle. This first one is dedicated to my oldest son, Tyler.

Fly, Arrow, Fly!
(2001, 41 years old, for my first son, Tyler, at his baptism)

Carefully, God reached down
and placed you in my arms.
"Love, cherish and raise him.
And keep him from all harm."

Like Joseph, the father of Jesus,
I knew my role for you
was to raise you as best as I could
until you knew your Father true.

So, I held you in my arms,
so near and close to my heart,
and made sure you knew where you came from
right from the very start.

We played football, basketball and more
under the hot, Florida sun,
until one day you were bigger and stronger—
and could beat me one on one!

Like the man after God's own heart,
we prayed like David you'd be.
And like the man for whom you were named,
is the man who stands before me.

Tall, strong and handsome
(you take after your mother).
And as an arrow in mid-flight,
Satan is soon to shudder.

Like arrows in the hands of a warrior
are my sons born to me.
Three weapons to fight for the right—
three sons of destiny!

So, fly arrow, fly!
Fly fast, straight and true.
And rescue the souls in darkness
that are waiting there for you!

Fly, arrow, fly!
Into the heart of the spiritual war!
See what adventures await you,
what victories are in store!

Fly, arrow, fly!
Back to your roots and sod.
Over and over repent
and come back to the heart of God.

Fly, arrow, fly!
Fly past me, straighter and farther!
Fly for the glory of God
until you reach your heavenly Father!

A university professor today, my third son, Ryan, has always had an uncommon aptitude for insight and analysis. Those natural abilities, coupled with a soft heart, made him an extraordinary youngster whose spiritual giftedness was apparent at an early age. One day, five-year-old Ryan brought me an unusual acorn in the shape of a heart. I was busy on my computer at the time, and thoughtlessly dismissed his spiritual vision as a mistake. But his insistence on the specialness of his treasure made me do a double take and realize it was I who had been mistaken. This poem recalls that indicative event.

> *"Each of you should use whatever gift you*
> *have received to serve others,*
> *as faithful stewards of God's grace*
> *in its various forms."*
> (1 Peter 4:19)

An Arrow to the Heart
(2005, 45 years old, for my third son, Ryan, at his baptism)

Only a boy of five years old,
and already
the sacred truth
you told:
"Look, Daddy, a golden heart."
"It's only an acorn"
I said with a start.

But with gifted vision from above
you whispered softly
with the greatest love:
"No, Daddy, it's a golden heart."
And from my eyes
the scales depart.

The acorn was more
than my eyes perceived
when your insight
my soul received.
And from that day
you've restored many more
whose vision was weak
and needed faith restored.

From demons in trees
to us on our knees
we looked through the veil
and saw the realities
of angels and demons,
Satan and the Lord,
forever bonding us
with spiritual cords.

At the perfect time
and the perfect hour,
the cross broke your heart
and your tears showered.
Dunked in the waves
at a California beach
your fingers touched
and the Lord you reached!

And the arrow was fired
across the starry sky—
angels and demons all wide-eyed
as it left the hand
of Our Shield and Rampart,
emblazoned with the words:
"An arrow to the heart!"

Now the demons cringe
and fear for their lives.
Any fear in your heart
is only their lies!
So, fight on your knees
until the Sprit imparts
that fire from above
that you had from the start!

His aim is true
and this they knew.
That's why they fought,
and still fight you.
But always remember
that God's set you apart
to be a blazing arrow—
an arrow to the heart!

This poem refers to when my second son, Kyle, was almost hit by lightning. He was ten years old when he and his friend, Trent Conkling, were canoeing in a lake close by the house. Suddenly, a lightning storm approached and they knew they had to get out of the water. These afternoon storms are common in South Florida where we lived at the time. What was uncommon was that, after the two of them put their roller blades back on and quickly skated home, a lightning bolt struck the tree just outside our house, knocking Kyle over. The tree died, but Kyle was unharmed. Adventurous and risk-taking, this memorable event seems to capture the spirit of my second son.

"He fills his hands with lightning
and commands it to strike its mark."
(Job 36:32)

The Arrow Flew and Flew!

(2007, 47 years old, for my second son, Kyle, at his baptism)

I pulled with all my might,
making sure the aim was true,
then watched in sheer amazement
as the arrow flew and flew!

It flew into the sky
and pierced the umbrella blue—
my son had become a man
before I even knew.

It seemed like only yesterday
they were in that green canoe,
paddling with all their might,
dark storm clouds in view.

Then swiftly onto land they jumped
and skated home, it's true,
hoping to outrace the lightning
thunderously crashing through!

Kyle and Trent would never forget
the fire that God threw.
It burned our tree and would have him,
if not for Kyle's shoes!

What message of divine power
was in that celestial clue?
Was it a warning, or a sneak preview
of all that he would do?

Smart, strong and handsome—
the world awaits his debut.
What has God prepared for him?
What will this young man do?

He of whom the lightning spared,
to give him life anew—
what adventures still await him?
What maiden will he rescue?

Who knows what God has planned
for Kyle to break through?
What battles will he fight?
What demons will he subdue?

Heroic arrows were once young too—
their exploits small and few.
But once in the hands of God,
no arrow flies untrue.

Tonight, the arrow flies—
all the way to heaven's dew—
as Kyle Chacon is baptized,
and with God's life imbued!

So, tonight we celebrate
along with heaven's crew,
as this precious child of God
is born to Him anew!

Chapter Eight:

Falling Deeper in Love with God

My 40s and 50s
2000 – 2020

The screenshot on my phone is a picture of my wife. It's not a wedding photo or a special occasion. It's just a picture of Lisa, sitting on a dining room chair and looking at me with loving eyes. I love that picture. It warms my heart every time I look at it. I can't tell you why. All I know is there's something about her face that's inviting to me. She's my home, and I feel safe, secure, and loved when I'm with her.

Faces reveal a lot, and eyes are windows to the mind. That's why I want to see God's face. I've given him my heart; I've left everyone and everything to follow him. I love him. And he loves me—more than anyone's ever loved me. Through thick and thin, and all my ups and downs, he's always been there for me. He's truly become my closest relationship.

But I can't see him. I can't touch him or hold him or feel his loving arms around me. And that frustrates me. But one day, he will look at me with the most loving eyes I have ever beheld, and he will hold me and comfort me. I know that I am fully known and fully loved. And one day, I will see the face that exudes that. And so will you...

"Now we see but a poor reflection as in a mirror;
then we shall see face to face.
Now I know in part;
then I shall know fully,
even as I am fully known."
(1 Corinthians 13:12)

"They will see his face..."
(Revelation 22:4)

His Face

(2000, 40 years old)

I know what I want.
That's what happens when you get older—
you begin to eliminate options.
The more mistakes you make,
the more options you begin to eliminate,
until your focus becomes narrowed,
and then, eventually,
that focus becomes singular.

Clarity of purpose produces incredible energy.
Someone who knows what they want
will stop at nothing to get it.
Their hunger becomes selective and intensifies.
Do you know what you want?
What will you stop at nothing to get?
What are you hungry for?

I know what I want.
I want to see God's face.
When it's just he and I together, all alone,
just the two of us.
I want to see him.
I like to read about him and I like to hear about him.
But I long to see him,

to look into his eyes as he looks back at me,
and to know him, as he knows me.

That's what I want.
He knows that.
I've told him several times.
Many times, when it's just been he and I together
in one of our favorite prayer spots
I've begged him:
"Come on, just once, let me see you."

And he wanted to do it.
Even now he longs to show himself to me.
In fact, I picture him straining to hold back!
But he doesn't do it.
He won't show me his face.
Even though he longs to do it.
And I long to see it.

But that just makes our desire increase.
One day, one very special and glorious day,
he will do it.
He will reveal himself to me—
and I will see him—face to face.
I long for that day.
I live for that day—
when I shall behold him,
face to face…

ave you ever thought of God as beautiful? Beauty is not skin deep, but includes all the elements of a person's mind, body, heart, and soul. We've all known physically attractive people who are not beautiful people. And we've also known physically unremarkable people who exude beauty from within. I believe God is incredibly beautiful—from the symmetry of his perfectly balanced character, to the qualities of his purest heart, to the magnificence of his royal bearing. I have no doubt that the God you and I love and walk with is the most stunningly beautiful being in the universe. I can't wait to see him.

> *"Your eyes will see the king in his beauty."*
> (Isaiah 33:17a)

> *"One thing I ask from the Lord,*
> *this only do I seek:*
> *that I may dwell in the house of the Lord*
> *all the days of my life,*
> *to gaze on the beauty of the Lord*
> *and to seek him in his temple."*
> (Psalm 27:4)

> *"And I—in righteousness I will see your face;*
> *when I awake, I will be satisfied*
> *with seeing your likeness."*
> (Psalm 17:5)

How Beautiful is God?
(2012, 52 years old)

What creative artist
painted the blue-green water of Maui,
the earth tones of the Redwood Forest,
and the multi-colors of a rainbow?

What thunderous personality
made the Amazon River,
Victoria, and Niagara Falls?

What majestic nobility
made the Rocky Mountains,
the Alps, and the Himalayas?

What intelligence and power made
"The Whirlpool Galaxy"—
31 million light years away from earth
and containing 300 billion stars!

What wildness of heart
made the African Serengeti
with lions, cheetahs, and elephants?

What free spirit
made wind, waves,
and the animals that ride them?

What passionate heart
came up with the idea of
music, rhythm, and dance?

What romantic heart
made a kiss so delicious,
and lovemaking so enjoyable?

What is the stunning form
of he who shaped
the form of a woman?

What is the look on the face
of him who is
love incarnate?

The greatest promise of God
is that one day
we will see Him—
face to face!

This is what we long for!
This is what will finally and fully
satisfy our deepest desires!

Seeing and knowing
God in heaven
will bring ultimate
and ongoing satisfaction—
forever!

Chapter Nine:

Helping Others Grow

My 40s – 50s
2000 – 2020

I was hired as the new minister for a church that had been growing numerically for several years under the previous minister. Unfortunately, the church had also lost many of their new converts, including most of the teens who had thrived in the frenetic energy of the exciting teen ministry, but then left their faith behind as soon as they went to college or moved somewhere else. It was a clear case of rocky soil that had no root:

"Others, like seed sown on rocky places,
hear the word and at once receive it with joy.
[17]But since they have no root, they last only a short time.
When trouble or persecution comes because of the word,
they quickly fall away."
(Mark 4:16-17)

So, I began preaching sermons about Jesus and some of the deeper truths of the faith to guide them toward maturity. Many thrived, but one prominent lay leader was frustrated with me and my new approach. He sat me down one day and said, "Look, here's how it works: you tell us what to do, and we go do it." I was stunned. Is that how he saw my role as the minister, and his role as a member? Is that how he viewed Christianity? A congregation needs practical guidance and assistance, for sure. But our programs must help members to better follow Jesus himself, or they will be outwardly obedient to the program, and not inwardly following the Lord.

My heart ached for those who see Christianity in such transactional terms, and in my longing for them to experience greater depth in their personal walk with God, I wrote this poem...

Just Tell Me What to Do
(2001, 41 years old)

I won't tell you what to do
but I'll show you who to follow
so your lives will be fulfilled
and your souls no longer hollow.

Jesus gives us life
and fills our days with wonder!
But man gives only rules
that tear our hearts asunder.

"Return to little children"
is what Jesus had to say.
Live from your hearts -
that's the better way!

But men want rules to follow
like Pharisees of long ago,
so we don't have to think and feel—
just put it on cruise control.

"Just tell me what to do.
I like it better that way.
Don't ask me to follow my heart.
My heart has led me astray."

But with visions of Jesus in mind
it can be different this time.
Just set your hearts above
and the path will surely shine!

Jesus said, "Follow me,
and we'll teach others to follow."
But put the cart before the horse,
and religion will soon be hollow.

Abundant life awaits
all those who live from their hearts!
It's harder to do, for sure—
but that's when the Spirit starts!

Look to Jesus today!
Let go the rules of men.
Come back to the heart of God,
and let's start over again!

I won't tell you what to do,
but I'll show you who to follow
so your lives will be fulfilled
and your souls no longer hollow.

*H*ow would it change your life if you could see the spiritual beings who interact with you each day? How would it affect you to see the hulking figure of a demonic figure climbing on your back and weighing you down? Or the seductive figure of a persuasive demon egging you on toward the addictions that enslave you? Think I'm crazy? Read your Bible. The same book that speaks of God and his angels also speaks of Satan and his demons. You cannot believe in one without also believing in the other. And if you only believe what you want to believe, you're a casualty of war already. Don't be naïve…

"Your enemy the devil
prowls around like a roaring lion
looking for someone to devour."
(1 Peter 5:8)

Your Enemy
(2001, 41 years old)

He's your worst nightmare.

He's more cunning than a serial killer,
more dangerous than a terrorist,
and more powerful than all the armies of the world
combined.

He's sneaky, underhanded and covert.

He is the demise of many a good man, woman,
and nation.

He is very good at what he does.
In fact, he's the best.

He's a killer, a liar and a thief.
But most people never even know
that they've been taken by him.

You have...

He's stolen your purity,
damaged your relationships,
and crippled your walk with God.

He's been in your house,
in your car,
in your bedroom,
and in your heart.

He fights dirty,
hits below the belt,
and doesn't play by the rules.

He has one goal in life:
to destroy you
and everything that you love
and hold dear.

And he won't stop
until he sees you burn in hell—
for eternity.

What is his name?

He is called Lucifer or Beelzebub,
the ruler of darkness,
the prince of this world.

He is called Belial, Abaddon, and Apollyon.

He is called the god of this age.

He is our accuser, our adversary, and our enemy.

He is referred to as
the great dragon,
the serpent,
the tempter,
and the evil one.

He is the angel of the abyss,
the prince of demons,
the ruler of the kingdom of the air...

He is the devil.

And his name is Satan.

*I*t's one thing to know that we have an enemy who hates us and is trying to destroy our faith. It's another thing to be aware of how he is trying to do it, so that we can be on our guard against him. God's Word warns us that our enemy is "crafty" (Genesis 3:1) and devises "schemes" to ensnare us (Ephesians 6:11). Some of those crafty schemes can even involve speaking to us through other people. Jesus immediately recognized the voice of Satan when Peter tried to dissuade him from going to the cross:

> *Jesus turned and said to Peter,*
> *"Get behind me, Satan!*
> *You are a stumbling block to me;*
> *you do not have in mind the concerns of God,*
> *but merely human concerns."*
> (Matthew 16:23)

The following poem is about doubts. There's nothing wrong with doubt itself. In fact, doubt that leads to examining our faith more closely is an essential part of developing our own faith. But doubt that leads to weakening or abandoning our faith can be from Satan. Like Jesus, we must discern where the voices we hear are coming from, even when they are in our own heads. That's the warning of this next poem...

Trick or Treat
(2007, 47 years old)

The trick is to make you think it was your idea.

That it was you who started having doubts about your faith;
That it was you who couldn't seem to get them out of your
mind— especially when you started to pray.

That it was you who started to mock your own prayers,
making you feel silly for speaking into the air.

The Tooth-Fairy, the Boogey Man, The Easter Bunny, Santa Claus,
and now this... maybe it's time to grow up.

"Give it a try," you *thought* you said to yourself.
"You don't need that crutch any more.
Try it for an hour.
Then try it for a day.
You can do it!
You're stronger than you think."

You see, the trick is to make you think it was *your* idea...

when it was actually *him* all along...

"Trick or treat"

*You've **been** tricked.*

Chapter Ten:

Reflections on the Journey

My 60s
2020 – Present

*J*t's easy to seek praise and avoid criticism from others—that path is wider and easier to follow. Conversely, the path of living to please God is narrower and harder to follow—but it's also immensely satisfying. I'm still growing in this area, but the more I disassociate myself from the evaluation of others, the better off I am. The scripture below even calls us to not judge ourselves, but to wait for the Lord to judge us, since he knows us better than we know ourselves. When we disassociate ourselves from the evaluation of people, and simply seek to please God, we will find it strange that man is so prone to heaping both excessive praise and excessive blame on us—when all we're trying to do is follow the Lord.

> *³I care very little if I am judged by you*
> *or by any human court;*
> *indeed, I do not even judge myself.*
> *⁴My conscience is clear,*

but that does not make me innocent.
It is the Lord who judges me.
⁵Therefore judge nothing before the appointed time;
wait until the Lord comes.
He will bring to light what is hidden in darkness
and will expose the motives of the heart.
At that time each will
receive their praise from God."
(1 Corinthians 4:3-5)

Follow the Flame
(2020, 60 years old)

They shared at his baptism
and called him a hero
for coming so far
when starting at zero.

But to him it was strange
that they applauded his name
since all he had done
was to follow The Flame.

They called him a troublemaker
when he raised his hand
to seek where the Lord
would want us to stand.

But to him it was strange
that they ridiculed his name
since all he had done
was to follow The Flame.

They loved being taught
with spiritual wisdom
when he preached his insights
about the kingdom.

But to him it was strange
that they applauded his name
since all he had done
was to follow The Flame.

They questioned his motives
and accused him of pride
when he stepped up to lead,
the church to guide.

But to him it was strange
that they ridiculed his name
since all he had done
was to follow The Flame.

Throughout his life
he heard both praise and ridicule
from those whose affections
would both heat and then cool.

But to him it was strange
they even mentioned his name—
since all he ever did…
was to follow The Flame.

I recently read that we make about 35,000 decisions a day. I don't know, seems high to me. But either way, that's a lot of decisions, and I'm sure I make a lot of wrong ones every day. But here's the thing: as I look back on my life, there's one decision I'm sure I got right—and that's the decision to follow Jesus. I made Jesus the Lord of my life on May 10, 1981. I've seen the fruit of that decision over four decades and I believe it's the best decision I've ever made in my life. The key is to stand by it.

Peter denied the Lord and had to be restored to that relationship. Jesus restored it, and then called Peter to follow him to death. Peter followed, and the rest is history. No matter how many times we fall and get back up, may God give you and I the grace to stand by our decision to follow him, all the way to the end.

"Very truly I tell you, when you were younger you
dressed yourself and went where you wanted;
but when you are old you will stretch out your hands,
and someone else will dress you and
lead you where you do not want to go.'
[19]Jesus said this to indicate the kind of death
by which Peter would glorify God.
Then he said to him,
'Follow me!'"
(John 21:18-19)

Where You lead, I Will Follow
(2020, 60 years old)

When the signs of the times are confusing,
and I don't know which way to go—
where you lead, I will follow.

When the fear of getting cancelled is lurking,
and one wrong word is a deathblow—
where you lead, I will follow.

When words exchanged left me bleeding,
and my heart is pierced with an arrow—
where you lead, I will follow.

When the slavery of my idols is mocking,
and my sin has left me hollow—
where you lead, I will follow.

When the clouds of my tears are blurring,
and they fall like rain on my pillow—
where you lead, I will follow.

When my troubles seem to be multiplying,
and I could sure use a hero—
where you lead, I will follow.

*a*s a follower of Jesus, I want so badly to be the best representative of God that I can possibly be. He deserves that. But often my flaws, shortcomings, and inadequacies feel like disqualifications to me. And then I reflect on my spiritual ancestry and realize that all my biblical heroes felt the same way: Moses, David, Peter, etc. All of them felt inadequate. As Paul said, when speaking of our mission to present Christ to others, *"And who is equal to such a task* (2 Corinthians 2:16b)?" And so, we press on, not with confidence in ourselves, but with confidence in his promise to be with us and work through us. And I have found his promises to be trustworthy.

> *But Moses said to God,*
> *"Who am I that I should go to Pharaoh*
> *and bring the Israelites out of Egypt?"*
> *12And God said,*
> *"I will be with you."*
> (Exodus 3:11-12a)

Who Are We?
(2021, 61 years old)

We walk with a limp, like Jacob—
and yet, we walk.

We speak with faltering lips, like Moses—
and yet, we speak.

We fall into sin, like David—
and yet, we get back up.

We get depressed, like Elijah—
and yet, we rise.

We deny Christ, like Peter—
and yet, we are restored.

We get distracted, like Martha—
and yet, he always brings us back.

We get frustrated in ministry, like Paul—
and yet, we continue to give our hearts.

Who are we?

We are flawed and feeble people—
called to be representatives
of the one who
turns our weakness into strength,
and never leaves our side.

Who are we?

We are his people.

Epilogue

I know this might sound unusual, but I honestly feel like this is not my book; it's God's book—the book he is writing with my life. He planned it all: from my birth and pre-Christian life, to the circumstances of my conversion, to my continued growth in Christ. This is his book. I am his book.

> *"You show that you are a letter from Christ,*
> *the result of our ministry,*
> *written not with ink*
> *but with the Spirit of the living God,*
> *not on tablets of stone*
> *but on tablets of human hearts."*
> (2 Corinthians 3:3)

So, what book is God writing with your life? What's the arc of the story? Who are the main characters along the way? What are some of the key lessons learned? Reach out to me and tell me. I'd love to hear your story. And be sure to tell others. Tell your family, your loved ones, and the people God puts in your path. Testimonies are powerful; that's why the Bible is full of them. And God wants our lives to testify to his faithfulness.

This last poem is from a conversation I had with the Lord on one of my prayer-walks last year. (No, I don't hear from him all the time, and no, it wasn't audible. But I believe our Creator can easily coordinate communication with his creations any time he chooses. This was one of those times.)

The conversation is about where I go from here. I don't know what will come next for me, but I know one thing: I'm determined to follow Christ wherever he leads me. I will walk the path he's set out for me. And by his grace, one day that path will lead me all the way home. I'll see you there.

"Walk the Path"
(2022, 62 years old)

I asked Jesus
what word he had for me
and he said,
"Walk the path."

I asked "How?"
And he said,
"Do what's set before you."

He said,
"Do not shrink back,
do not get distracted,
and do not turn to the right or to the left.
Do what's set before you.
That's how you walk the path."

I said,
"I will".

And he said,
"I know you will."

Acknowledgements

There are so many men and women whom God has used to help shape my spiritual life over the last four decades. But I want to particularly acknowledge these profound influences on me:

John Godwin and Gary Sorenson, who led me to Christ.

Gordon Ferguson, who taught me God's grace.

Gregg Marutzky, who taught me God's wisdom.

Bruce Williams, who taught me how to be a man of God.

Mike Rock, who taught me how to love God from my heart.

Robert Carrillo, who is like a brother to me, and always speaks to my heart.

Rob Zabala, who inspires me with his deep passion for God.

Ron Conkling, who inspires me with his heart to do what's right.

Daren Overstreet, who feels like a brother from another mother.

My brother-brothers: Chris, Paul, and Ralph, with whom I have a special bond.

My other half, Lisa, who knows and loves me like no other.

My three grown sons: Tyler, Kyle, and Ryan, who have truly become my best friends.

My three daughters in law: Tiffany, Amanda, and Andrea, who have made my sons so happy.

My eight grandchildren: Finn, Sophia, Lily, Justus, Mila, Julie, Ava, and Desmond, who bring me more joy and delight than I can possibly express.

Through their public ministries, some of my treasured teachers and counselors: C.S. Lewis, John Piper, Timothy Keller, Frances Chan, John Eldredge, and John Mark Comer.

And to many, many more whom God has put in my life—I am eternally grateful.

About the Author

Jeff Chacon served in the full-time ministry for 36 years before retiring in 2022, and now serves as an elder for the Anchor Point Church in Tampa, Florida. Jeff and his wife, Lisa, are probably most well known for their marriage and family workshops, as well as Jeff's first book, *Dare to Dream Again.* They have three amazing sons, three wonderful daughters-in-law, and eight adorable grandchildren.

Dare
to Dream
Again
Getting Back Up When Life Knocks You Down

Jeff Chacon

Available at www.ipibooks.com

Books available at

www.ipibooks.com

Books available at

www.ipibooks.com